Spooky fun

Marion Haslam

p

This is a Parragon Publishing Book
This edition published 2002

Parragon Publishing
Queen Street House
4 Queen Street
Bath BA1 1HE, UK

Designed, produced and packaged by
Stonecastle Graphics Limited

Written by Marion Haslam
Edited by Philip de Ste. Croix
Designed by Sue Pressley and Paul Turner
Craft items by Marion Haslam
Photography by Roddy Paine
Styling by Sue Pressley and Paul Turner
Face painting on pages 18 and 19 by Caro Childs
Games illustrations by Terry Longhurst
Additional line drawings by Malcolm Porter

ISBN 0-75258-692-0

Printed in China

Author's Acknowledgements
Many thanks to Dylon and Sia for supplying craft
materials and props for photography.

Disclaimer
Halloween should be fun, but safety is very
important. Young children should always be
supervised by a responsible adult when
making the craft items or food and drinks
described in this book. Naked flames,
Halloween games and trick-or-treat activities
should be supervised by an adult. Face
painting: always use proprietary face paints
specifically designed for face painting and
follow all safety instructions. Always check
that your model does not suffer from any
allergies. Do not paint children under two
years old or anyone who has a facial cut, sore
skin or sore eyes. The publisher and their
agents cannot accept liability for any loss,
damage or injury however caused.

Contents

Spooky Halloween facts

"Trick-or-treat!" Think of Halloween, and it's likely that you will immediately bring to mind the practice of trick-or-treating when children dressed in costume go from door to door asking for gifts and treats.

It's great fun and a marvellous opportunity for putting on some spooky outfits. There are many popular events associated with Halloween, such as pumpkin carving and trick-or-treating.

How it all Began

The holiday we now celebrate as Halloween on 31 October has a long history, dating back more than 2000 years. It is a combination of Celtic, Roman and Christian festivals which have all merged over the years. For the Celts, 1 November marked the start of their new year and the winter months were known as the season of darkness.

In a three-day festival, spirits and ghosts were invoked as it was believed that the veils between the spirit world and the living world were at their thinnest at this time of year. After hundreds of years, these autumn festivals also featured bonfires and people dressed up as saints, devils and angels. Through the ages this developed into All Hallows Eve on 31 October – what we now call Halloween.

Well, that's the end of the history lesson! Now let's enjoy this season with its ghosts and ghouls and celebrations of light and darkness. It's time to dip into *Spooky Fun* and conjure up the spirit of Halloween!

Q. What kind of beans do cannibals like best?

A. Human beans.

Q. Where do vampires send their dirty clothes?

A. To a dry screamers.

Materials

The projects in *Spooky Fun* are designed to use everyday things around the house and in many cases the same raw materials are used again and again. It is a good idea to set up a creative materials box, so that you can enjoy a weekend of making things without having to stop to go out and buy essential bits and pieces. Useful items include the following:

Paper

Start collecting papers, such as sugar paper, art paper and crêpe paper. You should also save tissue paper and ribbon used as gift wrapping, plus cellophane and foil candy wrappers as they are always useful for decoration.

Template Plastic

In order to use the templates at the back of the book, you will first need to trace them. You can buy clear template plastic in various sizes and cut it with scissors to create long-lasting templates.

Paints and Brushes

Poster paints are great all-round paints and they usually come ready-mixed. They are easier to use if you pour a little onto a saucer. Acrylic paints can also be used for a wide variety of crafts. A pack of brushes of assorted sizes is a good idea. Always wash your brushes after use so that they will last longer in good condition.

Scissors and Cutters

Have a pair of both large and small scissors, and, if you are planning to sew, a separate pair of fabric scissors. Craft knives with retractable blades should only be used by older children. Always use them with a cutting mat so you do not gouge the tabletop!

Glue

Choose a craft glue which dries clear. PVA glue can be watered down when gluing tissue and used as a "varnish." Glues which come in a pot with a brush are handy. You can also use cotton swabs as a glue brush when you have to glue a small item (such as wobble eyes).

Tape

A clear sticky tape and a reel of masking tape are suitable for many projects.

Pipe Cleaners

These are usually sold in packs and are available in jazzy colors as well as black and white.

Pom Poms

You can make your own, but this is quite time-consuming. They are inexpensive to buy in multi-packs of various sizes.

Craft Wire

Often used for jewelry making, a reel of craft wire is very useful for tin can votives.

Kebab Skewers

These oversized toothpicks are really useful, so buy a pack when you are helping with the weekly shop!

Thread and Shirring Elastic

Keep reels of thread in black, white and a few other colors handy, plus of course some needles and a reel of shirring elastic.

If you are searching for other materials, look in your local art shop and supermarket for many of the supplies you will need.

Q. Who did the ghost take to the movies?

A. His ghoulfriend.

Halloween Crafts

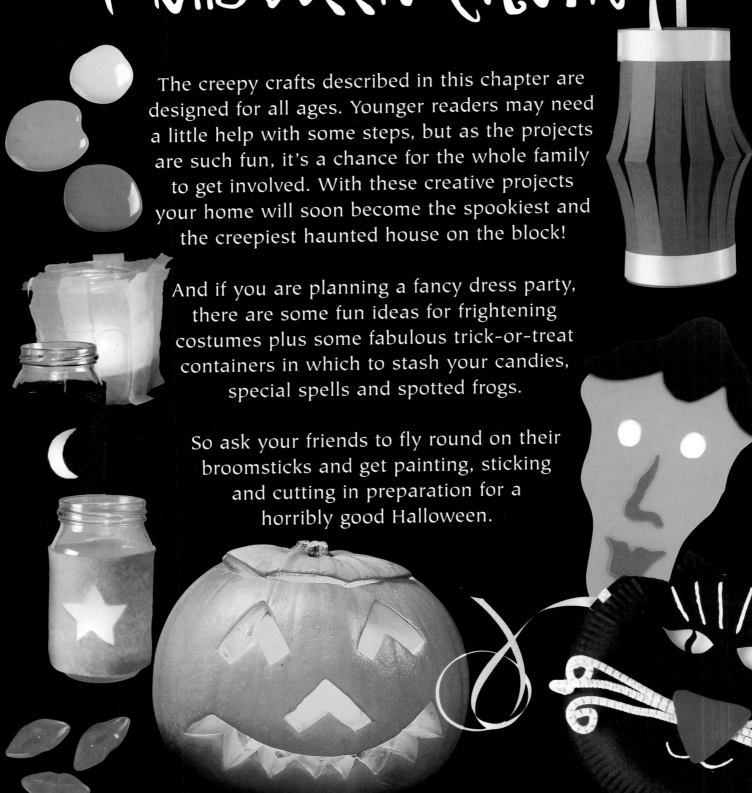

The creepy crafts described in this chapter are designed for all ages. Younger readers may need a little help with some steps, but as the projects are such fun, it's a chance for the whole family to get involved. With these creative projects your home will soon become the spookiest and the creepiest haunted house on the block!

And if you are planning a fancy dress party, there are some fun ideas for frightening costumes plus some fabulous trick-or-treat containers in which to stash your candies, special spells and spotted frogs.

So ask your friends to fly round on their broomsticks and get painting, sticking and cutting in preparation for a horribly good Halloween.

Q. What does the sign say in front of ghost washroom?

Q. Boils and Ghouls!

Creepy Costumes

EVERYONE NEEDS a costume at Halloween – there is a lot of spooking and shrieking to be done when trick-or-treating and at parties.

Costumes can be expensive to buy or hire, but everyday clothes can easily be recycled and disguised as the garb of warty witches, marvellous magicians and gruesome ghosts.

And the good news is that you can create a deliciously horrible outfit in no time at all.

The essential ingredients are usually some sweatshirts and pants, colored pantyhose, plenty of crêpe paper, clothes dye, a little imagination and a big sense of humor.

When making costumes, very little or no sewing is the order of the day. The one point to remember is that costumes and cloaks should not be so long that you trip over them. So cut them off a few inches above the ground.

Pumpkin

The jolliest costume of all has to be a Jack o' Lantern as you have to be bright orange. Or if green is your favorite color, go as a gourd instead! In fact gourds, although very similar to pumpkins in many ways, can be almost any shape, size or color. Gourds can sometimes be very very knobbly – so woolly pantyhose to show off your knees would be great!

One option is to dye a bedsheet bright pumpkin orange, cut a hole in the center for your head and wear it as a tunic. You can add details with fabric paints. Wear green or brown opaque pantyhose. Add a collar of leaves made from crêpe paper or attach them to a green baseball cap.

Another completely wild idea needs a hula hoop, several packets of orange crêpe paper and someone to help you get dressed!

1 Make sure you wear a layer or two of warm clothes.

2 Make a collar out of rolled-up crêpe paper and fasten it around your neck.

3 Cut two lengths of string to act as braces and attach them to the hula hoop, so that it hangs from your shoulders at hip level.

4 Cut off long strips of paper about 4in wide which are long enough to reach from the collar over the hula hoop to just above your knees.

5 Attach the strip to the collar, let it hang over the hula hoop (you may need some sticky tape to secure it) and let it drop.

6 Attach the second strip in the same way until you are completely wrapped up. You will be the plumpest pumpkin in town!

Skeleton

Wear long black sweat pants and a long-sleeved turtle neck sweater. Your bones can made from a number of materials – sticky-backed felt or plastic, white drinking straws, torn-up sheeting and bandages are just some options.

Stick or safety-pin them to your outfit. However, the easiest solution is to use old clothes which can be painted with white fabric paint. This allows you to position the bones just where you want them.

Remember to stuff the clothes with newspaper as you paint them, so that the color does not bleed from the front to the back of the material. Wear a ski mask or balaclava to cover your face.

Q. What did the father ghost say to the baby ghost?

A. Don't spook until you're spooken to!

Monster

The main trick for creating wicked monster-wear is to use bold and clashing colors – monsters are not subtle! Costumes made from fleece or sweatshirt material are ideal for outdoor trick-or-treating as they are warm.

Use fleece or sweatshirt tops and shorts in bright colors, colored pantyhose, squares of bright colored felt, a hairband, pipe cleaners, white pom poms, scraps of black felt.

Using round objects such as cups for templates, draw different sizes of circles on the felt square. Cut out and position them on the front of the fleece top. Pin them in place and sew on with running stitches. (You can easily unpick these later if the top needs to be worn again.)

Make a triple eyeball hairband, by twisting the bottom 2in of the pipe cleaners around a hairband. Glue white pom poms to the top of the pipe cleaners and glue a small circle of black felt onto each pom pom. Leave it to dry before wearing.

alternatives

- Make arm scales by cutting felt or fleece into large triangles and tacking them onto the underside of sleeves.
- Make a swishing tail by stuffing one leg of an old pair of brightly colored pantyhose. Use the other leg to wrap around your waist and tie in place.
- Decorate shoes with a cuff of brightly colored crêpe paper tied around the ankle. Cut two strips of crêpe paper, 2 and 4in wide.
  Pleat them and then attach around the ankle with sticky tape.

Vampire

Vampire capes are cheap to buy but you could rustle up your own vampire costume in the dark of night.

Wear a red or white top and black trousers (Tip: if the clothes have motifs or logos, turn the garments inside out to hide them.) Make a cape from a 55in square of black skirt-lining satin and buy the same size of plain red fleece. Attach the two at the neck edge with a strip of stick-and-stick Velcro and secure around the neck with another piece of Velcro, remembering to leave a collar upstanding. You could wear black or red gloves and add a set of rubber fangs. For even greater effect, make your hair stand up in peaks with some stiff hair gel and you are ready to suck some blood.

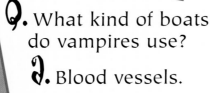

Q. What kind of boats do vampires use?

A. Blood vessels.

Q. What is Dracula's favorite fruit?

A. Necktarines.

Little Devil

If you like red, this outfit is for you! The main requirement are red clothes and a large red cloak.

Make horns by sticking a pipe cleaner between two pieces of felt cut into horn shapes, which can be wound round a head band.

Cut a three-pronged spearhead from a black piece of thin cardboard and stick it to a wooden dowel or length of garden bamboo.

Ghost

Getting dressed as a ghost is as easy as pie. All you need is a white bedsheet, white cheesecloth or a sheet of glasshouse frost protector from your local garden shop (very cheap and large).

Don't forget to cut holes for your eyes and wear some warm clothes underneath as sheets can be drafty! Another option is to wrap and drape a sheet around you and cut holes in a white pillowcase to wear as a hood.

Wizard

Wizards look wonderful in purple and gold. Cut stars and moons from gold paper and attach them to a cloak. Dye a nightdress purple and decorate it with old Celtic symbols using glitter paint. Add a conical hat made from thin purple cardboard, a book of spells and you are ready to make magic.

Spider

As spiders come in all colors of the rainbow, you have plenty of options! All you need is a leotard and pantyhose and four extra legs! Make these from two old pairs of opaque pantyhose. Stuff each leg with newspaper. Roll over the hip section and pin it to your back. A balaclava or ski mask adds the finishing touch.

And don't forget that masks and face painting can help make even the simplest outfit look convincing...see pages 18 and 19.

Witch

All you need is black, black and more black! Old clothes can easily be dyed in the washing machine with clothes dye.

Skirts can be short or long – stripy pantyhose are ideal. Add oversize cardboard buckles (painted a gold color) to black boots or shoes.

A cloak is a must – choose a square of fleece for trick-or-treating, or satin lining material for parties (or you could dye some sheeting). Other essential ingredients are a conical black hat, a broom and a black cat. And lastly do not forget some dark lipstick, painted nails and a fearsome cackle.

Q. How do witches like to drink their coffee?

A. From a cup and sorcerer.

Q. What does a witch ask for when she is in a hotel?

A. Broom service.

Q. Why do witches ride on broomsticks?

Q. Because vacuum cleaners are too heavy.

face Painting

Create the finishing touch to your Halloween costume with simple face painting techniques.

Ghoulish Ghost

This design is easy to do and very effective, but remember, you are only wearing face paint, so don't try walking through walls!

You will need
• Plenty of white paint and some red, purple, and black • Sponges • A large piece of white material

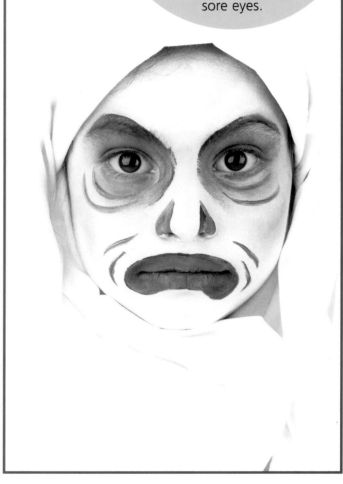

1 Ghosts may come in many shapes and forms, but a typical spook is very pale, so take a sponge with plenty of white paint on it and sponge a smooth base all over the model's face.

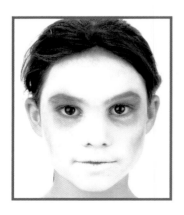

2 Rub your white sponge into some purple paint and gently blend purple around the eye sockets and under the cheekbones.

3 Rub the sponge into some red paint and make the color around the eyes a deeper reddish-purple. Paint dark lines under your model's eyes.

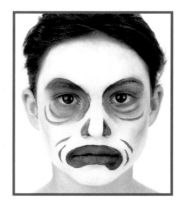

4 Use a large paintbrush to paint a sad wailing mouth. Use black paint or purple and red mixed together. Finish the disguise by draping a bedsheet or some spare white material over your model's head.

Vlad the Vampire

The vampire spends the daylight hours sleeping in its coffin but at night it can flit like a bat, searching for innocent victims who have forgotten to hang garlic around their necks.

You will need
Black, white, and red paint • Sponges • Paintbrush

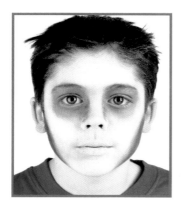

1 Sponge a white base all over the face, then, with a little black on the sponge carefully create some shadows by lightly sponging the eye sockets, the sides of the nose and the cheeks. You can make these shadows more definite by painting a line and then pulling the paint away from it with a sponge, but it looks more natural if you can do them freehand.

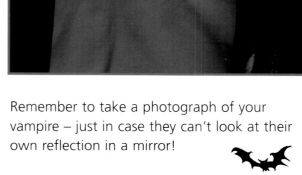

2 Sponge a little red below the eye and onto the cheeks.

Remember to take a photograph of your vampire – just in case they can't look at their own reflection in a mirror!

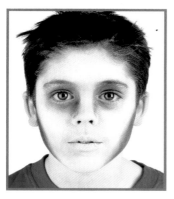

3 Paint a black triangle with the point downwards in the center of the hairline and sponge black paint into the hair around the face. Don't worry, face paint washes out easily. Now paint in dark eyebrows.

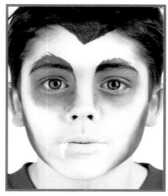

4 Use a clean brush to paint white fangs at the corner of the vampire's mouth.

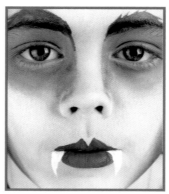

5 Mix up a dark red with a little black in it and use this to paint pointy lips.

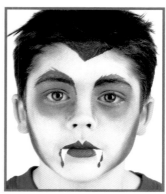

6 You can add some drops of red paint to represent blood dripping off the teeth.

Window Decorations

These quick-to-make decorations can hang in your windows, on door handles or from the banisters.

Bobbing Furry Spider

Bessie the black widow spider has been busy eating fly pie and yet that glint in her eye means she's still a little hungry… I wonder where her husband is?

You will need
- 12in pipe cleaner
- 2in black pom pom
- 1in black pom pom
- Needle • Black thread • Scissors • Craft glue
- 39in black shirring elastic
- Pair of 3/8in wobble eyes

1 Tie a knot at the end of the thread. Cut the pipe cleaner into four equal lengths to make four sets of legs. Bend each pipe cleaner in half to make a pair of legs and sew each pair onto the pom pom. Bend the pipe cleaners to make knees and feet.

2 Sew the smaller pom pom (the head) onto the larger one. Make a knot in the elastic and then thread the elastic through the head.

3 Glue on the bobble eyes and when dry, hang your fat, juicy spider somewhere to scare the arachnophobes (that's spider-haters to you and me)!

Floating Ghosts

Suspend these ghosts where they will catch drafts of air and so float around. These are instant spooks, literally made in seconds. You can see them again on page 11.

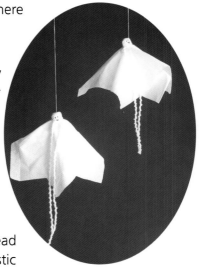

You will need
- White 2-ply tissue
- Black pen
- 1/2in cotton craft ball
- 15in white yarn or thread
- 30in white shirring elastic

1 Take each tissue and peel the two layers apart. Place the layers on top of one another to make an eight-pointed shape. Place the cotton ball at the center and pick up the tissue holding its ball head in the middle.

2 Place the elastic so that about an inch hangs down at the back of the head. Tie the length of yarn tightly around the bottom of the head. This secures the tissue and the elastic at the same time.

3 Draw eyes and a mouth on the head and then suspend your spook.

TIP!
You can make a tasty alternative suitable for trick-or-treat and party bags if you use a wrapped lollipop instead of the cotton ball.

Sparkling Witch Balls

Sparkling Witch Balls were extremely popular in England during the 18th century. These hand-blown glass globes were hung in peoples' homes at the window. It was believed that they attracted witches' spells and evil spirits. Once inside the ball, the spell or spirit was trapped and could never escape, so protecting the families in their homes. Make your own interpretation to glint and glow in the window, rather like a stained glass mobile.

You will need
- 12in pipe cleaners
- 4$\frac{1}{2}$in x 4$\frac{1}{2}$in colored cellophane sheets
- Needle and thread • Scissors

1 Twist each pipe cleaner into a circle and overlap the ends by $\frac{3}{4}$in. Twist the ends back onto the circle and adjust the shape as necessary.

2 Prick a hole in the cellophane square, about $\frac{1}{3}$in from the edge. Cut off a long length of thread, knot it around the first circle and then thread it through the cellophane hole. After about 6in, tie the thread around the second pipe cleaner circle and slip on a different color cellophane square. Continue until your string of "witch balls" is long enough to hang in a window where the light can gleam through the cellophane as it twists and turns.

TIP!
Cellophane is used for wrapping candies. However, rather than ruining your teeth in an attempt to get enough cellophane for this project, you can buy pre-cut squares in packs from specialist kitchenware suppliers!

a Haunted Village

Place this haunted village on a table or windowsill to create an instant chill down the spine. As it requires some patience to cut out the details, the project is best suited to older children.

You will need
- 300g weight art card in a dark color • Ruler
- Pencil • Scissors • Craft knife • Cutting mat

1 Enlarge the template on page 62 to the size you want on a photocopier and cut out the outlines.

2 The village shown here measures 28 x 11in, with each house 7in wide. Measure your houses and village as they are on your photocopy. Cut a rectangle of card to the size of the whole village and draw a line to indicate the folds between the houses.

3 Using the photocopy, mark the outlines of the roofs and the positions of the doors and windows on the card. Cut out carefully. You will need to use the scissors plus the craft knife and cutting mat.

Some of the windows are left as shutters, so only cut these on three sides and then bend the card back to make the shutter.

TIP! When using scissors, make a small cut at the center of the shape with the craft knife, to allow you to get the scissor points through the card. Make a snip out to the edge of the shape or a corner. This will help you to get sharp corners and even lines.

4 Fold the card into a zigzag shape and stand it where light (such as a table lamp) falls from behind or to the side of the village. The shadows will make the houses look even spookier.

TIP! When folding the card, place a ruler against the fold line and bend the card up against the ruler. This produces a clean, sharp edge.

Spiders' Webs

In the fall, spiders' webs are everywhere. You can easily make your own by following these ideas.

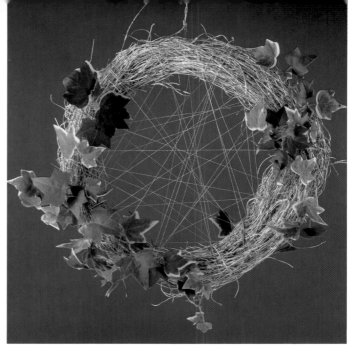

Sparkly Web

Spray a twig wreath with silver paint. Wrap metallic embroidery thread around the wreath and decorate it with ivy. Hang from the front door with a Bobbing Furry Spider (see page 20) to scare visitors!

Wire Web Mobile

Bend two metal coat hangers into rough diamond shapes and wire them together with craft wire. Wrap more wire into the spaces and suspend tissue ghosts and paper spiders from the lower hook and wires. Hang the wreath up from the other hook.

Flytrap Web

This project is suitable for older children. Some spiders have special bristles on their back legs which they use to comb their silk into a sticky, woolly mass to trap flies. Take four lengths of craft wire, each about 24in long, and twist them together at the center, so that you have eight radiating spokes. Take another length of wire and twist it round each spoke to create the web, making at least three rows of cross threads.

When the wire runs out, just twist another length onto the end and carry on. Don't worry if the web twists out of shape – just bend it back! Stretch out a length of fluffy white yarn and tie it between the spokes. Glue on spider confetti or joke flies and hang the web from the ceiling above eye level (because of the wire spokes) where it will catch a draft and spin around.

Outdoor Cobwebs

If you have a metal gate or fence, get some white yarn and loop it around the metal bars to make an oversized spider's web.

To make it really scary, make sure you attach a bobbing spider (near to the gate handle)!

Votive Holders

Knock knock.
Who's there?
Thumping.
Thumping who?
Thumping green
and thlimy ith
crawling up
your neck.

Jolly Jars

Wash out empty jars and soak off the labels, before dressing them in their Halloween finery.

• Cut a length of orange felt long enough to wrap round the jar. Cut a Halloween shape such as a star, hat or pumpkin out of the felt and glue it to the jar. You could also use a hole punch to punch out a border of holes.

• Glue strips of torn tissue paper in contrasting colors to the jar to create a stripy light. As tissue paper is so thin, use PVA glue which can be watered down.

• If using poster paints for other projects, pour a little paint into the jar, dilute it with water and paint the inside of the glass. The paint will run down and look messy, but when a tealight is placed inside, the effect is a gentle glow.

• Stick confetti onto the outside of the jar. Make a collar for the jar out of a rectangle of heavy tracing paper, the same height as the jar and slightly bigger in circumference, so it slips easily over the jar once the ends are stuck with tape. The slight gap between the glass and the paper magnifies the confetti shapes.

TIP! Preserve jars often have curved bases. To make sure that the tealight is level, first pour in some sand, rice or lentils which will create a flat base for the light to sit on.

24

Hollowed out apples

Get back to nature with these fruity tealight holders. Ask an adult to help you cut the bottom off some firm red apples to create firm bases. Carefully hollow out the insides so that a tealight will fit snugly inside each apple. Sprinkle some cinnamon or nutmeg into each apple before inserting a tealight. Ask an adult to place the apples somewhere safe before lighting them. As the wax melts and the apple warms, a lovely aroma will fill the room.

Punched tin Lantern

Recycling garbage has never been such fun! Old tin cans are converted into great lanterns using ice, a hammer and a nail. You will need to ask an adult to help you.

Wash out an old tin can. Do not use one with rough edges, or you may cut yourself. Fill with cold water and freeze. Once frozen, stick a length of masking tape around the tin and draw a simple dotted pattern. Using a folded bath towel as a cushion, rest the tin on its side. Taking a hammer and nail, place the nail over the first dot and hit about six times to punch a hole. Repeat along the tape and make a second line of holes further up the can. Punch two holes near the open end of the can. Melt the ice, dry and thread a length of ribbon or craft wire through the holes to form a handle.

Candle and Light Safety

Light and candles are an important part of the Halloween tradition as a reminder that the nights are lengthening as winter approaches and also that light wards off evil spirits (think of vampires who only go out at night). However, you must remember that candles are naked flames, so follow these sensible guidelines:

- Never place or light candles or tealights near to paper decorations.

- Never leave lit candles unattended.

- Ask an adult to light candles (parents – keep matches out of reach of small children and buy extra-long candle matches to make lighting tealights in holders easier).

- Tealights should always be placed in a suitable holder.

- If you are illuminating the garden for your Halloween party, never place candles or tealights close to paths or doorways as your party guests may be wearing long costumes which could brush against them and catch light.

- If using fairy lights to decorate the garden, make sure that they are suitable for outdoor use.

Q. What do you get when you cross a vampire and a snowman?
A. Frostbite.

Q. Why are vampires artistic?
A. They are good at drawing blood!

Quick and Easy Paper Plate Masks

3 Cut out eye shapes and mouths if you wish (younger children may need help with this). Use a black pen to add other features.

4 Attach a length of ribbon to either side and tie the mask around your head. Alternatively, take a length of elastic and attatch it to each side of the mask. You can tie a knot in the elastic at the back to ensure a really secure fit.

You will need:
- Paper plates • Poster paint • Paintbrush
- Scraps of paper or pipe cleaners to decorate
- Craft glue • Scissors • Black pen
- 32in ribbon

1 Paint the underneath of your paper plate and leave it to dry.

2 Cut out shapes from the paper to add leaves or wings to your mask as appropriate.

TIP! If you are making a spider or a cat, cut pipe cleaners into lengths and stick them onto the mask. It is a good idea to curl the ends into spirals so that the sharp ends cannot hurt anyone.

Q. What do you do with a green monster?

A. Wait until it ripens.

Q. What days of the week do skeletons like best?

A. Moonday, Tombsday and Frightday.

Q. Why do mummies make excellent spies?

A. They are good at keeping things under wraps.

Q. What do you call three ghosts in a belfry?

A. Dead ringers.

Spooky Lighting

Keep the darkness at bay with some great lighting ideas to scare away the demons, witches, and black cats.

Jeepers Creepers

Make this spooky eyes lightshade and hang it from the ceiling wherever you want someone to watch over you! The light source is a snap stick available from camping shops. These sticks are completely safe to use. You simply snap the plastic tube and the stick gives off a green or yellow light for up to 12 hours.

You will need
- Black art paper • Pencil • Scissors • Sticky tape
- Scraps of tissue paper • Small black stickers
- 4 kebab skewers • Thread • Camping light stick

1 Cut four rectangles 6 x 10in from the black paper. Draw a pair of spooky eyes onto each rectangle. Cut out the eyes but remember to leave a small strip of paper between overlapping eyeballs.

2 Stick on small pieces of tissue paper to cover the eyes. On the right side, stick a black dot onto each eye to look like a pupil.

3 Take two kebab skewers and make a cross with them. Using a length of thread, tie them securely together so that the cross is firm. Repeat with the other two skewers.

4 Punch a small hole at the center top and bottom of each black rectangle and thread the four sides of the cover onto the skewers. Snap the light stick and hook it over the center of the top skewers. Hang in position and shiver with fear!

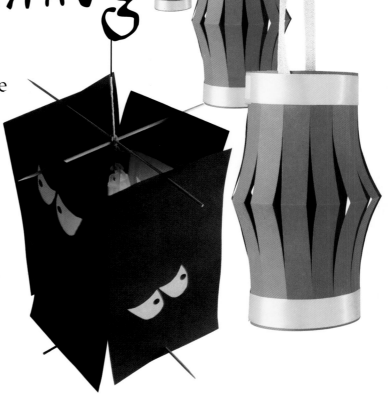

Chinese Lanterns

These are very quick and easy to make and are enjoyed by folk of all ages. Take a rectangular sheet of colored paper. Fold in half lengthways and cut from the center fold to about 1in from the edge. Make each cut about 1in apart. Open up and re-fold to form a circle. Overlap the ends and secure them with sticky tape or staples. Make two holes at the top and suspend the lantern from a ribbon loop. Hang the lanterns in clusters at different heights or string them in a line.

IDEAS!
Decorate the top and bottom edges with paint, stickers, metallic pens or papers. Make out of dark colored paper and decorate with glow-in-the-dark paint in spooky designs to hang outside.

Scary lights

Fairy lights turn scary with a Halloween makeover. Creepy collars in the shape of ghouls, bats and pumpkins create a fun, yet freaky atmosphere.

1 Using the templates on page 64, cut out shapes in art papers. (You do not need to attach one to every light for a good overall effect.) Cut shapes quickly by drawing round a template several times, then placing another strip of paper underneath to cut out two shapes at the same time.

2 Using a craft knife and cutting mat, make a small cross about ¼in long at the center. Add details in black pen if necessary. With a pencil push through the cross from the back to open up the hole. Push each collar well back over the light (it should not actually rest on the bulb). When lit, the scary lights will create spooky shadows on the shapes.

Q. Why did the monster eat a light bulb?

A. He was in need of a light snack.

31

Trick or Treat

Trick-or-treat, smell my feet.
Give me something good to eat!

When Halloween was still called All Souls Day, the poor would go through the town begging for food and promising to say a prayer for the dead if they were given a soulcake, specially baked for the day. Over time, the tradition was taken up by children and neighbors would give them candies, fruit or money rather than having a trick played on them.

If you are going trick-or-treating, you'll need something in which you can put all your goodies. If you are in costume, carry the theme through and decorate your basket or bucket in the same style. For tricks, why not make some extra tissue ghosts or write out Halloween jokes on paper to give away?

Ghost

Wrap your basket or bucket with white cheesecloth or use a white paper carrier bag and stick the letters BOO on the side in black paper. Put a camping light stick in the bag.

Skeleton

Carry a galvanized pail wrapped in ivy for a suitable graveyard look. Place a torch at the bottom of the pail for an eerie effect.

Witch

Make a cauldron out of a toy army helmet covered in black crêpe paper and tie a wooden spoon to the strap (handle).

Vampire

Cover a basket with red shiny fabric and tie an alarm clock to the handle to make sure you get back home before dawn!

Magician

Make a cone out of strong yellow or purple paper like an upside-down hat. Add a handle made from string or ribbon.

Pumpkin

Wrap a plastic bucket with polyester wadding or bubble-wrap to pad it out. Cover it with orange or green crêpe paper.

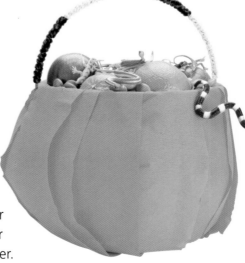

Halloween Safety

Trick-and-treating do's and don'ts

One of the most enjoyable aspects of Halloween is to dress up and go out knocking on neighbors doors "trick-or-treating." This can be pretty nerve-racking for parents, since during the rest of the year children are told "not to accept candies or talk to strangers." However, with a few simple precautions, everyone can safely have fun.

1 Always tell your parents before going out trick-or-treating and agree what time you will be coming home. Never go out on your own – always go with a group of friends (and preferably an adult). They won't spoil your fun as they will stay in the background. It is a good idea to take a cellphone with you, so you can call home if you need to.

2 Agree with your parents beforehand which roads you will be visiting. It is best to stay close to your home, as your friends and neighbors are more likely to be prepared with treats!

3 Don't split up – if someone wants to go home, everyone should walk home with them before continuing to trick-or-treat.
   (Parents – in order to encourage good group behavior, let your children know you have some extra treats on hand if they have to return early, provided they all come as a group.)

4 Make sure that you are warmly dressed (it is winter after all)! Pile on the layers under your witch and wizard costumes and remember that pumpkins and monsters are supposed to look plump! Use flashlights or light sticks when walking after dark.

5 Saty on the sidewalk and do not run out between parked cars. Remember that if you are dressed as black spiders and witches you will not be as easy to see as you would in your normal clothes. (Parents – think about sticking a reflective strip on the back of cloaks for greater visibility.)

6 Remember that not every neighbor will want to take part – do not pester them if they do not have treats and remember that older people may not open the door – respect their privacy. Say thank you!

7 Avoid houses with no lights.

8 If you are given unwrapped candies and you do not know the person that gave them to you, check with your parents first before eating them. (Parents – have some spare wrapped candies as a contingency in case you need to dispose of any dubious-looking treats.)

Have fun and don't eat all the treats at once!

PUMPKINS

It wouldn't be Halloween without pumpkins! It's easy to make great Jack o' Lanterns out of pumpkins, marrows or gourds. You will need to make paper templates and use a vegetable knife to cut out the shapes. Use an ice cream scoop or a melon baller to scoop out the insides of your Jack o' Lantern. Keep the flesh and seeds – you can use it all (see page 48 for pumpkin recipes). When the lantern is ready, ask an adult to light a tealight inside and watch Jack glow!

Tip! If you are a beginner at pumpkin carving, it is easier to use an apple corer for carving out circular eyes, nose and a big grinning mouth made from a line of holes.

DID YOU KNOW?

In 2000, Dave Stelts in Ohio, grew a pumpkin which weighed an incredible 1140lb.

That's an awful lot of pumpkin soup!

1 Make templates and draw around them in pen to create the face.

2 Cut a hole in the top with a vegetable knife and scoop out the insides.

3 Carefully carve out the shapes for the nose, eyes and mouth.

Q. What is a pumpkin?
Fruit? Vegetable? Animal?
A. Fruit

35

it's party time!

It's time to make things go bump in the night when you host a Halloween party! Parties at home in your own "haunted" house are ideal for letting children get slightly spooked within a safe environment and are a fun alternative to trick-or-treating.

Everyone can become involved from the moment of creating the party invitations to decorating the house. Making some gruesome gobbles to add a seasonal touch to normal party food is sure to produce plenty of shrieks from the junior chefs. Fancy dress is essential and many of the quicker craft ideas earlier in the book can also be included as party activities.

Remember that older children will find some games hilarious, whereas their younger brothers and sisters could be more easily frightened by the same activity. Think about this when inviting guests. It might be better to have an immediate "after school" party for 5–7-year-olds and another early in the evening for 8-12s.

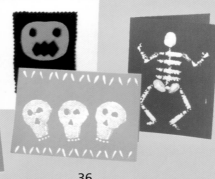

Q. What's huge and green and sits in the corner moaning all the time?

A. The Incredible Sulk

invitations

The fun starts here with a Halloween party! Set the scene with some great hand-made invitations for your friends. All these techniques can also be used for decorations, so be as creative as you like.

finger-Painted Ghosts

All you need is poster paint and a finger to create these ghostly heads. Once the paint is dry, you can draw spooky faces with black pen. Write in silver pen or attach a piece of white paper giving the party details.

Dancing Skeleton

Create a jigging skeleton with finger-painted skull and hip bones to start with. The rest of the bones are stamped with short lengths of pipe cleaner bent into an L-shape.

Ancient Chart

Dye some paper with cold tea to make it look old and then write out the party details, perhaps with a rhyme or a joke to spice things up. Tie up the invitation with some twine or seal it with wax.

funny fonts

Use the templates printed at the back of the book to cut out or color simple motifs such as bats and cats on cards. Use a funny font (typeface) on the computer to print out your details and attach the printed invitation and the shape to the card with glue.

Leo's Halloween Party

31 October at 7pm

at The Belfry, Church Rd

Do drop in
and hang around!

Jittery Jack O' Lantern

This is made from orange and black felt cut into a pumpkin shape and stuck onto a card with craft glue.

LET'S PARTY!

Confetti Caper

This idea is very quick and messy for the poor friend receiving the invitation! Write the details inside a plain card, leaving the front blank. Put the card into the envelope crease first and fill it with a handful of confetti. As the envelope is opened and the card pulled out, the confetti goes everywhere!

Witches & Warlocks

fancy Dress Party

on: 31 October
the bewitching hour: 7pm
at: 10 Forest Grove,
Sevenoaks

Q Why do black cats sing in a choir?
A Because they're very mewsical!

Potato Printing

Draw a simple design on paper. Cut a potato in half and draw the outline of the design on the cut surface. Trim out the background with a knife, leaving the raised design to be used as a stamp. Using a little poster paint poured into a saucer, stamp the design onto cards.

Glow-in-the-Dark invitations

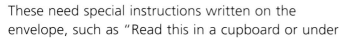

These need special instructions written on the envelope, such as "Read this in a cupboard or under your blankets!" Write the invitation onto dark colored card using glow-in-the-dark paint.

Puff Pumpkin

Use fabric paint to paint a simple design or message on a card. When dry, iron to puff up the paint.

Sticker Shriek

Another very easy invitation – use small stickers to spell out short words like BOO, EEK and HISS.

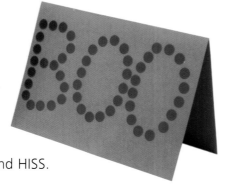

Shrunken Heads

Looking like wizened heads, these apples make great table decorations or they can be strung together to make a creepy garland. Make them at least a week in advance of Halloween to allow them time to shrivel!

You will need

- Firm apples – windfalls are fine • Paring knife
- Apple corer • Black pen • 1 cup of lemon juice
- 1 tablespoon salt • Toothpicks and a length of heavy string if you want to make a garland

1 Peel and core the apple. Using the pen draw facial features on one side – make them large as the apple will shrink as it dries out. Carve them out with a knife.

2 Pour the salt into the cup of lemon juice. Dip the apple into the juice solution – this will prevent the apple from turning too brown. Repeat with the other apples.

3 Leave the apples to dry out somewhere warm – above a radiator or in an airing cupboard is ideal. In a few days, the apples will shrink and shrivel and end up looking like wrinkled faces.

...t and fabulous ...corations

ow does a witch tell the time?

d. With a witch watch.

The Witches' Cauldron

Eye of newt, and toe of frog,
Wool of bat and tongue of dog,
Adder's fork and blind-worm's sting,
Lizard's leg, and owlet's wing,
For a charm of powerful trouble,
Like a hell-broth boil and bubble.

From *Macbeth* by William Shakespeare

Witch's Coven Window Silhouettes

Flying witches give a mysterious look to windows and for extra hubble and bubble add a cat and a witches' cauldron.

You will need
- Black paper
- Pencil
- Scissors
- Colored tissue paper
- Craft glue
- Sticky tape

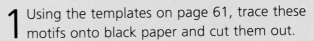

1 Using the templates on page 61, trace these motifs onto black paper and cut them out.

2 For small window panes, cut the tissue paper to the size of the glass. For large windows, use the whole sheet of paper (and position it where you like on the glass pane).

3 Using a tiny amount of glue, stick the black silhouette to the tissue. If you are using a large piece of paper, you can stick on several shapes. When dry, stick the tissue onto the window or frame, with the black silhouette facing into the room.

When there is a light on in the room and it is dark outside, the shapes will be silhouetted against the "colored" glass.

Starry Skies Hanging Salt Dough

You will need
- 2 cups of plain flour
- 1 cup of table salt
- 1 cup of water
- Paper clips

1 Put the flour and salt in a mixing bowl. Add about $1/2$ cup of water and stir thoroughly to mix. Keep adding a tiny amount of water at a time until the mixture turns from a crumbly mixture to a dough-like mix. Do not add all the water if you do not need to.

2 On a flat worktop, knead the dough mix with your hands for about 10 minutes by folding it over and over. Put the mix in an airtight container to rest for at least 30 minutes.

3 Take a paper clip and carefully snip through the sides, to create three small hooks. Repeat with another clip and put them in a pile on the side to use with each dough shape.

4 Pull off a chunk of dough, about the size of a orange. Using a rolling pin, roll it out on the worktop, picking up the dough and turning it around and flipping it, so that it doesn't stick. The dough should be no thicker than $1/6$in.

5 Using cookie cutters, firmly press out stars and moons. Carefully lift the shapes and, if necessary, neaten any rough edges with your finger. At the top of each shape, press a paper clip hook into the dough. Place on a baking tray and bake at 225°F for three hours. Turn off the heat and leave in the oven until cool.

6 Paint and varnish the shapes using acrylic or craft paint. Hang the decorations from varying lengths of ribbon attached to a line, or suspend them from a coat hanger to make a mobile.

Party Paper Chains

Decorate your home with these easy-to-make seasonal paper chains. You can use any simple Halloween motif – just choose an appropriate color of paper and away you cut.

You will need
- Large sheets of colored, black and white paper
- Pencil • Small scissors • Ruler • Pens • Sticky tape
- Extra items for decoration such as unspun yarn, wobble eyes and card

1 Trace off one of the motifs shown on page 62 onto a scrap of paper and cut it out to use as a template.

TIP! If you want to draw your own design, first draw a box in pencil. Your motif should fit in the box and there should be areas of the design on both the left and right sides which touch the edge. This is where the paper folds will fall and so will create the joined-up chain.

2 Cut off a strip of paper along its length. For the witch's hat and ghost, cut the strip about 5$\frac{1}{2}$in wide; for the pumpkin, 4$\frac{1}{4}$in and for the cat, cut a strip about 2$\frac{3}{4}$in wide.

3 Measure the width of your motif (or length if it's a cat.) Carefully fold the paper in a zigzag to this measurement.

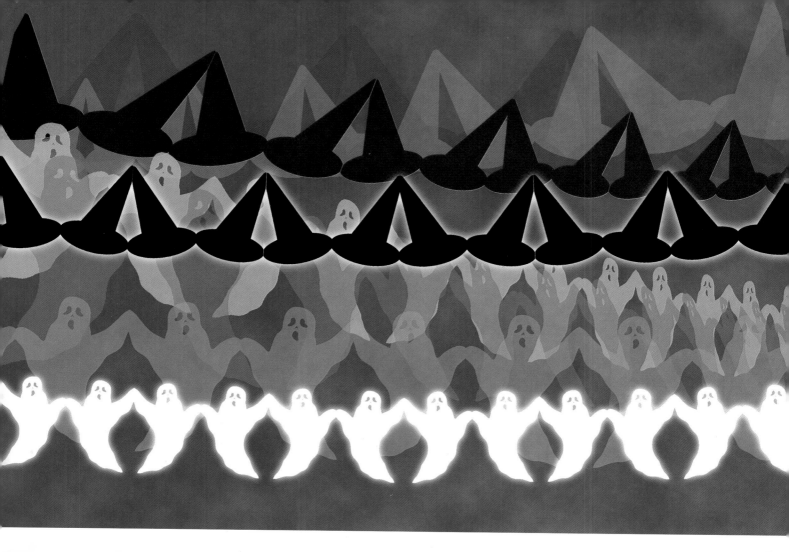

4 Place your template on top of the folded paper and trace around it with the pencil. Hold the paper firmly to prevent the concertina moving and cut out the shape.

TIP! Depending on the thickness of the paper, you will probably only be able to cut through five or six layers at a time. So cut out the top layers first and then repeat with the bottom folds. It is often easier to cut into a corner from two directions that meet at the corner.

5 Carefully open up the chain to check it is in one length! Make more chains and join them with sticky tape until it is the right length. Draw on details with a pen or stick on wobble eyes, pumpkin stalks or unspun yarn for witches' hair as you wish.

Witch's Brew

Eye of Lizard, toe of frog,
Tail of rat and bark of dog.
Sneeze of chicken, cough of bat,
Lick of weasel, smell of cat.

Stir it up and mix it well,
To make a magic
Halloween spell.

Scary Silhouette Placemats

Guests will love to have their own personalized placemat at the party table.

You will need
- Large sheets of art paper in a selection of colors
- Pencil • Ruler • Craft knife and cutting board
- Scissors • Masking tape
- Black pen • Gold, white or colored stickers to decorate

1 Cut a selection of the papers into rectangles 10 x 12in for the backgrounds.

2 On the wrong side of the placemat, draw out your Halloween motif using the templates on page 64. Keep the images simple and leave at least a 1in border all round.

Remember that the placemats will be used with the longest edge towards you (landscape), so draw the images this way round. However, you can always make the motif go from corner to corner like the bat.

3 Cut out on the line using a craft knife and mat, or scissors, whichever is easier.

4 Choose a contrasting color paper for the silhouette shape. Cut out a rectangle, large enough to cover the "hole" and stick it onto the reverse using masking tape.

5 Draw on details with pen or attach stickers to decorate. Write the child's name on the placemat.

Wanda Witch Name Cards

Wanda where you are sitting? Why not make tiny witch place cards for your party table which guests can take home when the party is over? You can quickly assemble a whole coven using old-fashioned wooden clothes pins (if you buy them from craft shops, they come with stands.) Decorate with scraps of black crêpe paper stuck on, plus odd bits of yarn and raffia. Make conical hats from semi-circles of black paper. Stick short lengths of yarn on the top of the clothes pin for hair or turn the pin upside down and thread raffia through the slit. Label the hats, thread names through the pegs or stand them on pieces of colored paper. And Abracadabra!

You can add a wizard as well!

Table Decoration Ideas

Use black and orange crêpe paper to cover the table in bold stripes.

Sprinkle plastic flies on the table. UGHH!

Make little bags of party favors by wrapping up jellied bugs, and black and orange candies in cellophane bags or crêpe paper and tying them with raffia or ribbon.

For older children, each paper napkin could be tied up with a length of ivy, and contain a Halloween joke and an indoor sparkler.

Potato-stamp a motif such as a witch's hat onto plain orange napkins.

Q. Why do witches wear name tags?

A. So they know which witch is which!

Spooky Savouries

Perfect Pumpkin Soup

This creamy, warming soup is prepared in minutes and serves four hungry adults as a main meal.

Ingredients

- 2lb of pumpkin, diced
- 1 large apple, diced
- 1 onion, chopped
- 1 carrot, sliced
- 1 stick of celery, sliced
- 2 garlic cloves
- 1oz butter
- 2pts chicken (or vegetable) stock
- Generous dash of green Tabasco sauce
- 2 bay leaves
- 1 branch of thyme
- 5fl oz half-fat crème fraîche
- 1/2 teaspoon nutmeg
- Salt and pepper
- Chives, chopped

1 Prepare the fruit and vegetables and crush the garlic.

2 Put the butter into the saucepan and sauté the vegetables and garlic for a couple of minutes. Add the pumpkin, apple, stock, tabasco, bay leaves and thyme. Bring to the boil and simmer for 20-25 minutes.

3 Remove the bay leaves and thyme and purée the soup in a blender until smooth. Stir in most of the crème fraîche and season with the nutmeg, a little salt and freshly ground pepper.

4 Serve with a dollop of crème fraîche or a few chopped chives in each bowl.

Witches' fingernails (Roasted Pumpkin Seeds)

1 Wash the pumpkin seeds and pat them dry with kitchen paper.

2 In a pudding basin, soak for about an hour in a little soy sauce.

3 Sprinkle with garlic powder if you wish and then sprinkle the seeds on a non-stick baking sheet.

4 Place in a pre-heated oven (225°F). After 30 minutes, turn the seeds over with a slice and continue roasting for another 30 minutes to one hour. When cooked, the seeds should be crunchy.

Witches' Fingers

Make chicken nibbles look like witches' hands complete with talons by cutting chicken breasts into curved slices, before stir-frying or coating and cooking them in breadcrumbs. Decorate with red pepper "fingernails" and serve them on a bed on noodles.

Creepy Kebab Broomsticks

Cut a square of black paper 2 x 2in. Snip a long fringe all along one side. With sticky tape, stick one end onto a kebab skewer. Wrap it tightly around the skewer and secure with another piece of tape. Tie a 4in length of raffia in a double knot at the top.

Make savoury kebabs by threading small cooked sausages, chunks of pepper, cherry tomatoes, cheese or mini corn onto the skewers. Sweet kebabs can be made from fruit, such as pineapple, melon, apple, banana and grapes.

Monster Pizzas

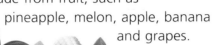

Decorate mini-pizzas with monster faces. Ideal ingredients include sliced stuffed olives for eyes, sliced peppers or pineapple for noses, sweetcorn for teeth and curly scallions for eyebrows. And remember that monsters can have three eyes, hundreds of teeth and goodness knows how many noses.

Beastly Biscuits

Jack o' Lantern Cookies

These chewy cookies have a scrummy spicy taste – very more-ish! This recipe will make 24-27 cookies.

Ingredients
- 6oz butter (softened)
- 3oz soft brown sugar
- 1/2 tin apple-pie filling
- 1 egg yolk
- 1 teaspoon vanilla essence
- Zest of an orange
- 12oz self-raising flour
- 1/2 teaspoon ground cinnamon
- 1/2 teaspoon ground nutmeg
- 2oz dried apricots for decorating

1 Preheat the oven to 375°F.

2 Cream the butter and brown sugar together. Add the apple-pie filling, egg yolk, vanilla essence and the orange zest. Mix thoroughly and set aside. In a separate bowl, combine the flour, cinnamon and nutmeg.

3 Gradually add the dry mixture to the wet mixture and stir until mixed. Place the cookie mix in a sealed plastic container and leave in the fridge for 30 minutes.

4 Remove the cookie mix and roll out the dough to a thickness of about 3/8in. Cut using a cookie cutter. Make a Jack o' Lantern face by pushing chopped apricot into the uncooked dough. Bake for 10 to 15 minutes and leave to cool on a rack.

Tarantula Treats

Ingredients
- Chocolate chip cookies
- 8oz chocolate
- Strawberry laces, cut into short lengths
- Tube of magic mushroom cake decorations

1 Break up the chocolate into chunks. Place in a heatproof bowl and melt over some gently simmering water.

TIP! Do not let the water splash into the bowl otherwise the chocolate is spoiled. It may be easier to melt the chocolate in two batches.

2 Dip the cookie into the chocolate. Fish it out with a spoon, let it drain for a few seconds and then place onto a sheet of baking parchment.

3 Lay four laces across the cookie like spider legs and stick two mushrooms onto the cookie as eyes. Leave the chocolate to set.

TIP! Sugared jellies also make great spiders' eyes.

Ghoulish Fairy Cakes

This recipe makes 12-15 cakes.

Ingredients
- 4oz self-raising flour
- 4oz butter or margarine, softened
- 4oz caster sugar
- 2 eggs, beaten
- A little milk

And to decorate
- 4oz confectioner's sugar, sieved and mixed with a little water for the icing
- Food colorings
- Strawberry preserve
- Jelly shapes

1 Put paper cases into a cake tin and preheat the oven to 375°F.

2 Cream the butter and sugar in a bowl until pale and fluffy. Add the eggs a little at a time, beating well.

3 Fold in half of the flour, using a tablespoon. Fold in the rest. If necessary, add a little milk to get a "dropping" consistency.

4 Fill each paper case two-thirds full and bake in the oven for 15-20 minutes until golden brown. Allow to cool on a wire rack before decorating.

Banana Bones

Cut bananas into slices about 3/8in thick. Push a banana slice onto each end of a white chocolate finger biscuit and make the biscuits look like bones good enough to eat!

To Decorate:

Devil's fangs: Spoon icing over the top of the cake and push in three or four jellied diamonds.

Spider's web: Spoon white icing over the cake. Pour a little food coloring onto a separate plate. With the paint brush, draw two circles on the icing and then using the knife, drag lines through the icing, alternating from the center and the outside edge, to give a cobweb-like pattern.

Bloodshot eyeball: Spoon white icing over the cake. Place half a glacé cherry at the center and then paint on red lines using the food coloring.

Dracula's blood: Using an apple corer, hollow out the center of each cake (not right to the bottom). Spoon in a little soft set strawberry preserve and replace the top of the cake. Spoon over the icing (dyed pink with a few drops of food coloring) and allow it to drip down the sides.

TIP! The icing solidifies quite quickly, so work speedily!

Q. What sauce does the skeleton like with every meal?

A. Grave-y.

Q. Why do demons go out with ghouls?

A. Because demons are a ghoul's best friend.

Putrid Puddings

Lizard Ice Bowl

This makes a fun serving bowl for scoops of ice cream. Make at least 48 hours in advance. Take two freezer-proof glass mixing bowls of different sizes – the smaller one should fit inside the larger to leave a 1in gap between the bowls.

1 Fill the larger bowl with cold water to a depth of about $1\frac{1}{2}$in. Sprinkle in some plastic lizards from a joke shop. Put in the freezer (make sure the bowl is level) and leave until frozen.

2 Remove from the freezer and place the smaller bowl on top of the frozen layer and weight it down. Pour in more water between the two bowls and add more lizards. Return to the freezer.

3 Once fully frozen, you can remove the inner bowl by wiping the inside with a cloth which has been run under hot water and then wrung out. Twist gently and the inner bowl will loosen. Remove the outer bowl, dip in warm water and twist again. Return to the freezer until needed.

Remember to place the bowl on a large plate as it will start to melt in a warm room.

Q. What do short-sighted ghosts wear?

a. Spooktacles.

52

Jellied bugs

Wobble with fear at this jelly containing gummy bugs. Make up a jelly according to the packet instructions. Sprinkle a few bugs into a glass bowl and pour jelly up to about a 1in depth. Place in the fridge to set, keeping the rest of the jelly at room temperature. Once set, layer more bugs and jelly into the bowl. Repeat this until all the jelly is used.

Gritty Graveyard Eyeball Trifle

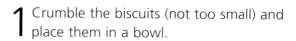

Ingredients
- ½ packet chocolate biscuits
- 5oz seedless grapes
- Packet of chocolate mousse powder
- Milk
- 12 sponge fingers

1 Crumble the biscuits (not too small) and place them in a bowl.

2 Cut the grapes in half and sprinkle onto the biscuits.

3 Make up the chocolate mousse with the milk and pour onto the grapes.

4 Insert the sponge fingers like tombstones around the edge of the bowl. (It doesn't matter if they tilt slightly.)

5 Poke a few chocolate finger biscuits at angles into the trifle to resemble dug-up bones.

Q. What does a cannibal get when he comes home late for dinner?
A. The cold shoulder.

53

Devilish Drinks

Warm Halloween Punch

This non-alcoholic punch is ideal for warming a skeleton's bones and witches' hearts after some trick-or-treating.

Pour equal quantities of orange juice, red grape juice, and of fizzy water into a large saucepan. Add slices of orange and lemon, a couple of cinnamon sticks and two mulled wine sachets. Simmer over a low heat until warm. Pour into glasses containing a metal teaspoon (so that the glass does not crack) and add golden raisins and almond flakes to look like more eyeballs and fingernails.

Q. What is Dracula's favorite kind of coffee?

a. Decoffinated.

Blood-Curdling ice Cubes

Add a few drops of red or green food coloring to a jug of cold water to color it. Pour the water into an ice cube tray and freeze it. If you half fill each section and freeze it, and then top up with another color, you will end up with red and green ice cubes. Watch your friends' mouths drop open when you fill their glass of lemonade with spooky ice cubes.

Witch's Brew

Chop up three apples into cubes. Make up a fruit punch with equal quantities of fruit juice, lemonade, and ginger ale. Add the cubed apples and some seedless grapes to look like teeth and eyeballs! Serve the wicked brew in encrusted glasses (see below) with creepy ice cubes and neon straws.

Encrusted Glasses

Color some white sugar in a glass jar by adding a few drops of green food coloring and shaking the mix vigorously. Pour a small amount of sugar onto a plate, dip the rim of a glass in some lemon juice and then dip it into the sugar to leave a light coating around the rim of the glass.

Apple Bobbing Game

This game is traditional at harvest time to celebrate a successful season.

Warning
This is great fun, very messy and wet. Have plenty of towels to mop up soggy party guests!

Cover the floor with a plastic sheet (or PVC tablecloth) to protect the carpet from water spills. Fill a large plastic bowl with water and place some small eating apples in the water (remove the stems to make the game harder).

Each child has to try and grab one of the apples from the bowl, using only lips and teeth and without using his or her hands.

If the bowl is big enough, have two players go at the same time, or alternatively time each contestant to decide who is the winner.

Gruesome Iced Hand

Color some water with food coloring and pour it into a disposable plastic glove. Leave the top 2in empty. Secure the cuff firmly with a bag tie and freeze, keeping the hand horizontal and the fingers separated. Once frozen, remove the tie, peel off the glove and add the disembodied hand to a bowl of clear water just before serving. Ughh!

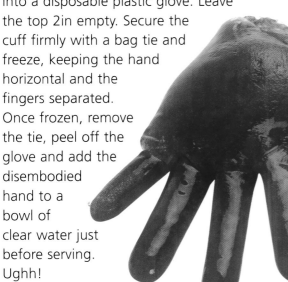

Toffee Apples

Crunchy toffee apples is a very old-fashioned recipe and the sweet, brittle toffee is a good contrast to the crisp, refreshing apple.

WARNING! This recipe should **ONLY** be tackled with the help of an adult because the toffee gets very hot as it is cooking.

Ingredients
- 6 medium-size, crisp dessert apples
- 14oz demerara sugar
- 1½oz butter
- 1 tablespoon vinegar
- 3fl oz water
- 1 tablespoon golden syrup
- 6 wooden sticks (lolly sticks are ideal)

1 Wash and dry the apples, remove the stalks and push a wooden stick firmly into the core of each apple.

2 Heat the sugar, butter, vinegar, water and syrup in a pan until all the sugar has dissolved. Bring to the boil, then simmer without stirring until the mixture reaches 350°F on a sugar thermometer.

3 Carefully remove the pan from the heat and plunge it into a bowl of cold water to prevent the toffee from cooking further.

4 Tilt the pan and taking one apple at a time, dip it into the toffee, twirling the stick until the apple is nicely covered with toffee. Place onto a baking tray and leave the toffee to set.

Q. What does the skeleton order at a restaurant?

A. Spare ribs.

Ghoulish Games

These fun ideas are great for making Halloween parties for all ages go with a bang or a shriek.

Web Weaving

This is a great icebreaker for children of all ages. You'll need odd balls of yarn, one for each player, so ask your knitting friends for their cast-offs or check the remnant bins in your local yarn or charity shop.

All the children should stand in a circle about 7-10ft in diameter. Give everyone a small ball of yarn which each child should tie around his or her waist. To start the game, shout

"My oh my, it's a fly! Start spinning!"

Each player should then toss the ball of yarn to another child (except their immediate neighbors). On catching the yarn, the child again loops it around his or her waist. Once everyone is ready, choose a child to shout the fly rhyme again and throw the balls a second time.

Repeat this about 10 or 12 times and the whole group will be tied up in a complex spider's web. When the game finishes, the first player to get themselves untangled (without resorting to scissors) is the winner.
WARNING
Do not allow the web to go around the players' necks as it could seriously hurt them.

Pin the Nose on the Pumpkin

Cut a large pumpkin out of orange-colored paper. Draw on the eyes and mouth with black pen and mark a small cross for where the nose should be. Pin the drawing on the wall. In turn give each child a small sticker with their initial written on it. Blindfold the child and turn them around three times while everybody chants:

"I'm a pumpkin, poor pumpkin, without a nose Nobody knows, where my nose goes"

The rather wobbly player then walks forward and sticks the sticker where they think the nose should go. The winner is the child whose nose is closest to the cross.

Torch Silhouettes

Using a torch try to create silhouettes with your hands of creatures (rabbits, mice, birds and frogs etc.) on the wall. The other children have to try and guess what the object is.

the Mad Scientist's Box

This game is great for older children and adults. The mad scientist has left his laboratory unlocked after working on his experiment to build a monster out of human and animal body parts. You have to guess what body parts he has left behind.

1 You will need a large cardboard box. Put it on its side with the flap left open. On the top cut a small hole, just big enough for a hand to pass through. You could cover or paint the box white and add a large red cross and labels saying "DO NOT TOUCH" and "ORGAN DONATION."

2 Place the "ingredients" on plates and keep them hidden from view by covering them with dish towels or kitchen paper. Have an assistant pass them to you in turn.

3 Each child has to put their hand in the hole, guess what the scientist has been using and write it down on a piece of paper without telling the others. It's a good idea to supply each child with a damp facecloth or piece of kitchen paper – this can get very messy!

Here are ideas for some Ghoulish ingredients:

Warm noodles – small intestines

Plumped-up golden raisins – dead flies

Skin off the top of custard – skin

Olives – eyeballs

Firm jelly – cartilage

1/2 piece of toast and some cornflakes – stomach contents

12in marabou trim – cat's tail

Flaked almonds – finger nails

Small orange (with hole created with apple corer) – eyeball socket

Bone from a chicken drumstick – any specified human bone

Jelly lips – mouth

Tomato ketchup – blood

Keep this until last!

Swamp Treasure

The old wizard has dropped his money bag into the swamp and needs help fishing out his treasures. This game can be used to award small cash prizes to winners of other games or as a game in its own right. Even without the buried treasure, it's an ideal pastime for wet days.

You will need 9oz of cornstarch, 1 pint of water, some green food coloring, a large mixing bowl, a spoon and a protective sheet of plastic or tablecloth. It's even better and slimier when the mix is made with double the quantities!

1 Pour a small amount of the cornstarch into the bowl, add some water and stir to mix. Keep adding more cornstarch and water, until all the cornstarch is mixed in (you may not need all the water). Add enough green food coloring and stir until it turns a swampy green.

2 Put some dimes or other small coins in the bowl (you may need to push them down well). Also put in some distractions like small beads or buttons.

3 Each child should roll up a sleeve and plunge a hand into the bowl, trying to grasp the buried treasure which has sunk to the bottom of the swamp.

Wait for the shrieks as the bowl appears to contains liquid, but at the bottom is a mass of gungey slime – yuk! If the child manages to extract a treasure, this could be exchanged for another small gift like a scrunchie, hair clips or candy.

WARNING! *When you have finished with the slime, do not pour it down the kitchen sink as it might block the drain. Put it carefully into a bag and throw it in the garbage can instead.*

The Witch's Spring Clean

This memory test is ideal for calming things down after a boisterous game such as web weaving.

On a large tray or on a tablecloth at the center of a table, place 15 items that a witch might have in her house. Include items such as: spectacles, a belt buckle, an emery board (ideal for filing those talons), a pot of cream labelled "wart ointment", a tin of cat food, a wooden spoon, a small preserve jar filled with colored water labelled "bat's blood", a candle, a pair of stripy pantyhose, plus some more unusual items that are not related to Halloween (dishcloth, pipe cleaner, magnifying glass, pebble, jar of spices etc).

Keep the lights fairly dim and let the children into the room to look at the objects for a minute.

Cover up the objects and give every child a piece of paper and a pencil. They have to write down everything that they can remember before the clock stops after five minutes. The winner is the person who remembers the greatest number of objects.

The Witch's Cauldron

This is a Halloween version of **"I went to the shops and bought a..."** word game which uses adjectives or alliteration within an ever lengthening list. The first child starts:

"The wizened witch stirred her cauldron and threw in...a spotted frog."

Everyone then repeats

"hiss, bubble and gulp."

The second child then repeats the introduction and adds another noun with an appropriate or alliterative adjective, such as

"...a terrified toad and a spotted frog...hiss, bubble and gulp."

Anything can be said, like

"a smelly sock," "a rusty bike."

The odder the better! As children forget the correct order of things, they drop out of the game.

Graveyard Unlucky Dip

This gruesome version of a lucky dip can be used to award small prizes for games. It is bound to produce squeals and shrieks! You can pitch the level of fright according to the age of the party guests!

YOU WILL NEED

- **Large cardboard box** – if you have time, cover it in woodgrain sticky-backed plastic to look like a coffin or paint it a dark color with poster paint
- **Dry crumbly garden soil or potting compost** • **Large pebbles**
- **Sheets of paper** – dyed in cold tea to make them look old • **Gruesome props** to bulk out the box and produce shrieks – plastic snakes, an old shoe, a sock, jewelry or a pair or glasses, cubes of jelly • **Paper and string** for wrapping up presents (black crêpe paper, bandages or newspaper obituaries for older guests) • **Ivy** from the garden (ask permission before you pick it!)

1 Write riddles or jokes on small pieces of tea-dyed paper and tie these onto pebbles as booby prizes. These could also be wrapped up to confuse anyone groping in the box.

2 Wrap up the prizes in your chosen wrapping.

3 Pour some soil or compost into the box. Lay in some ivy for tangling hands, some props and prizes and more soil. Keep layering the contents until the box is full. Put it on the floor on large sheets of newspaper – place in a gloomy corner so that guests cannot see clearly what they are picking up when they delve into the box.

idea!

If you have time, make a tombstone for the head of the box out of two large cereal boxes, glued together and covered in some layers of papier mâché, painted gray and wrapped in more ivy. Stick it to the end of the box.

"That girl over there just rolled her eyes at me"

"Well if you are a real gentleman, you'll pick them up and roll them back to her"

templates

Photocopy these templates to the required size.

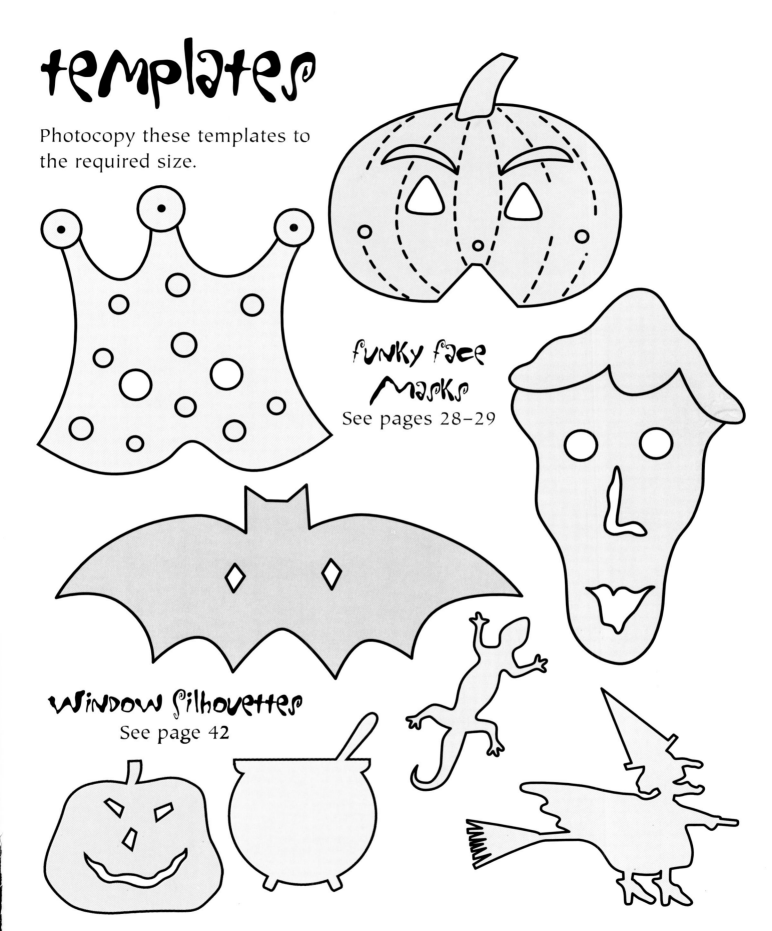

funky face
Masks
See pages 28–29

window silhouettes
See page 42

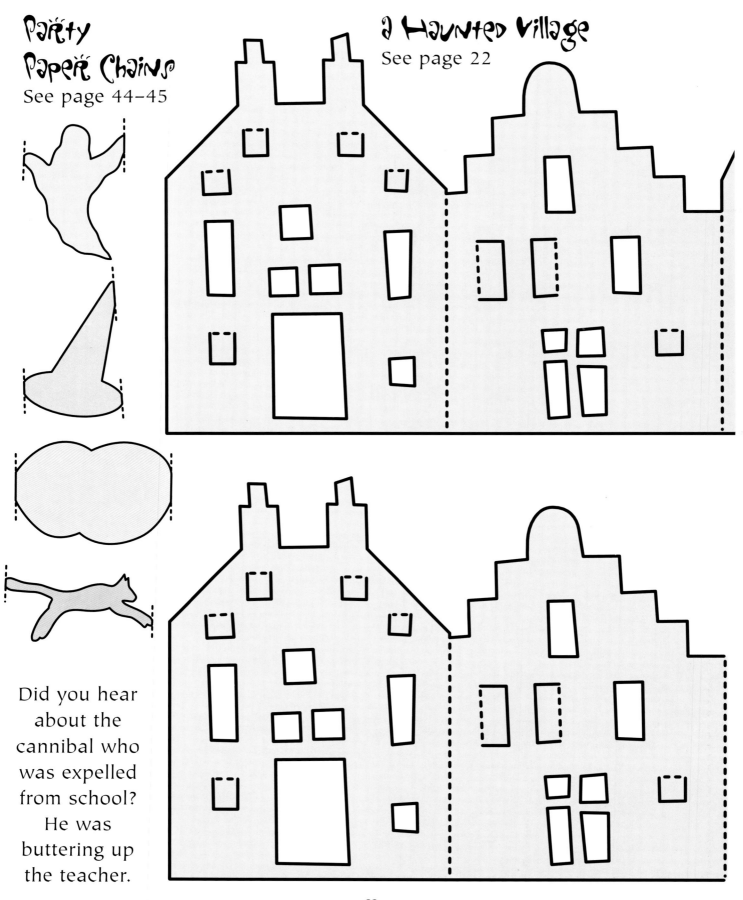

Party Paper Chains
See page 44–45

a Haunted Village
See page 22

Did you hear about the cannibal who was expelled from school? He was buttering up the teacher.

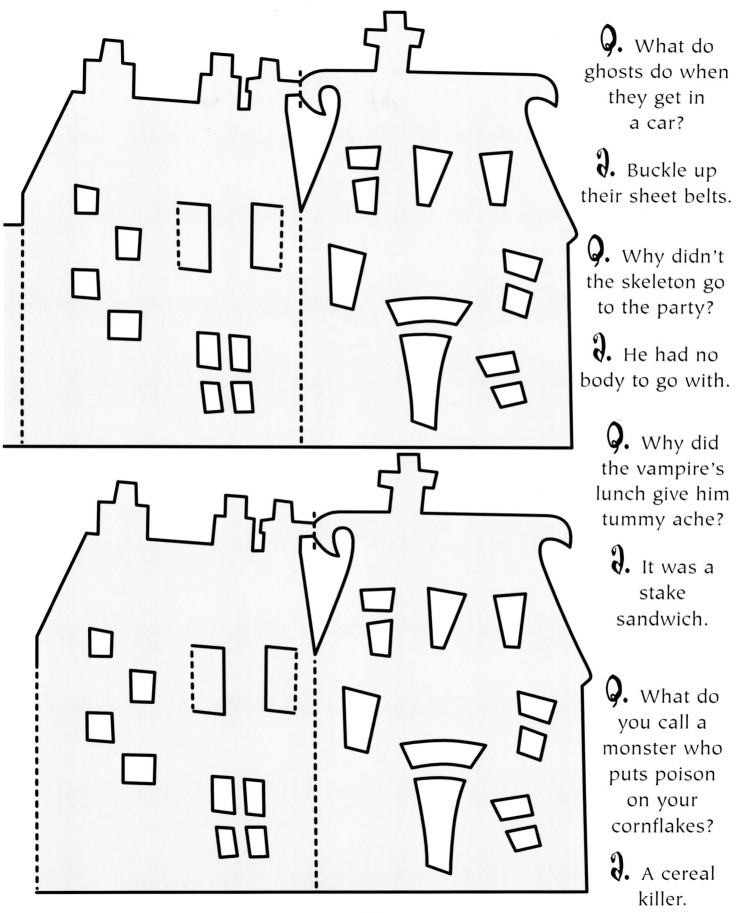

Q. What do ghosts do when they get in a car?

Q. Buckle up their sheet belts.

Q. Why didn't the skeleton go to the party?

Q. He had no body to go with.

Q. Why did the vampire's lunch give him tummy ache?

Q. It was a stake sandwich.

Q. What do you call a monster who puts poison on your cornflakes?

Q. A cereal killer.

63

Scary Lights
See page 31

Scary Silhouette Placemats
See page 46

Q. Why couldn't Dracula's wife get to sleep?

A. Because of his coffin.